Danah Haiz

Jonah's Journey

illustrated by H. Hechtkopf

Lerner Publications Company
Minneapolis, Minnesota

AN OUTSTANDING SELECTION FROM Israel

First published in the United States of America
1973 by Lerner Publications Company, Minneapolis, Minnesota

International Standard Book Number: 0-8225-0362-X
Library of Congress Catalog Number: 72-268

Printed in Israel and Bound in U.S.A.

Thousands of years ago, in the time when the Bible was written, there was a man named Jonah. Jonah belonged to the Hebrew people and lived in the land of Israel.

In the same time that Jonah lived, there was a great city called Nineveh. Nineveh was in the land of Mesopotamia, not far from Israel.

The people of Nineveh were very wealthy. They lived in large houses, they had many slaves, and they worshipped in great temples. The streets of Nineveh were filled with people from many nations. Some came to trade, some came to study, and others came only to see the city's beauty and wealth.

God loved Nineveh very much. He was proud that it was such a great city, and He was pleased by its beauty.

But God was angry with the people of Nineveh. They had turned to wickedness and did not obey God's laws. They had much money and many fine things, but they did not share with the poor people. They were talented, but they used their talents foolishly. God had given them many gifts, but they forgot to be thankful.

All these things made God very sad, and He knew the people of Nineveh would have to be punished.

One day God spoke to Jonah and said, "Jonah, I want you to go to the great city of Nineveh and tell the people there that I am angry with them. They have become very wicked and must be punished. Tell them that I am going to destroy Nineveh and all the people in it."

When Jonah heard these words, he was filled with fear. "This is terrible!" he thought. "I will be in great danger. How can the Lord ask this of me?" Jonah began to think of all the bad things that could happen to him. The journey to Nineveh would take three days, and he would have to travel up steep hills and through the desert. Robbers lived in the desert. The heat was unbearable. "And what if I do get safely to Nineveh?" Jonah thought. "Will the people there be happy when I tell them that God is going to destroy their city? No! They will be angry, and they will try to harm me."

Jonah decided to run away instead of going to Nineveh. He went down to the port of Joppa. At Joppa there were many ships from foreign lands. They sailed from Israel to all the countries around the Mediterranean Sea. Jonah paid the fare on a ship sailing to Tarshish, a city far across the sea. Then he took his belongings and hurried down into the ship's hull. Jonah thought he could hide inside the ship and run away from God.

After its cargo was loaded, Jonah's ship sailed toward Tarshish. At first everything was fine. The weather was good, and a steady wind filled the ship's big sail. The sailors hurried about, busy with their work. Some were sewing fishing nets and washing the deck, and others were watching the sails and guiding the ship. All the passengers walked around the deck, talking to each other and looking at the sea. All but Jonah—he did not leave the ship's hull.

After the ship had been at sea for two days, suddenly a storm came up. The wind was so strong that it rocked the ship back and forth. The passengers and sailors on the deck were blown off their feet. The sails ripped, and the masts splintered and broke. Huge waves crashed onto the deck and tossed the ship high into the air. "Help! Help!" shouted the watchman as he fell from the crow's nest to the deck. "We will all be killed!" cried a frightened passenger.

"Why didn't you tell us there was a storm coming?" the captain shouted at the ship's weatherman. "Were you sleeping instead of watching?"

"No, captain. No!" cried the weatherman. "Look! There is no storm. The sun is shining and there are no clouds. Something strange has caused this terrible wind."

The captain looked at the clear sky and the bright sun. It was true. There was no storm.

But the wind grew stronger and stronger. "This must be the work of some god," cried one of the sailors. Every man on the ship began to call out to the god he believed in. Everyone prayed and begged his god to stop the wind. The sailors threw their cargo overboard to lighten the ship. But still the wind rocked the ship, until it seemed certain to sink.

Then one of the sailors found Jonah in the hull, fast asleep on a bag of flour.

"What is this?" cried the sailor. "Why are you here? The ship is about to sink and you are sleeping! Call upon your god, as the rest of us are doing. Perhaps he will save us."

Then the captain said, "We will draw lots. Everyone on the ship will take a stone from this cup. One stone is black. We will find out which man has caused the wind—he will draw the black stone."

Jonah was terrified. He realized that the wind was his fault, but he didn't know what to do. When the lots were drawn, Jonah drew the black stone. Now everyone knew that he had caused the wind.

"Who are you?" the men demanded. "Where do you come from? What have you done to cause this trouble?"

Jonah answered them, "I am a Hebrew and I come from the land of Israel. I worship the Lord, the God of Heaven, who made the earth and the sea." Then Jonah told them the whole story, how God had told him to go to Nineveh and how he had run away.

"It is true," said Jonah. "This wind was sent because of me. The only way to stop the wind is to throw me into the sea. I am sure that is what the Lord wants."

When they heard this story, the sailors became frightened. They did not know about the Lord, and they did not want to throw Jonah into the sea. At first they decided not to believe Jonah. Instead, they took up the ship's oars and tried to row through the high waves. But the wind was too strong and their rowing did no good.

Next, the sailors decided to test Jonah's story. Two men held Jonah by his arms and lifted him over the side of the ship. As soon as Jonah's feet were in the water, the sea on that side of the ship grew calm. "Oh!" cried the sailors. "Can this really be happening?" Then the sailors lifted Jonah out of the water. At once the sea became rough, and high waves splashed up onto the deck. Again they hung Jonah over the side of the ship. As soon as Jonah's feet were in the water, the sea grew calm.

Now the sailors were more fearful than before. "His god does want us to throw him into the sea," they said. "We must do it or we will all be killed." But before they put Jonah into the sea, the sailors cried out to the Lord and asked Him to forgive them.

"We are only doing what you want," they said to the Lord. "Please don't punish us for killing Jonah."

Then they threw Jonah into the sea. Suddenly the wind stopped and the water grew calm. The sailors bowed down and worshipped the Lord. They knew He must be a powerful God.

When the sailors threw him off the ship, Jonah hit the water with a big splash. Then down and down he went into the sea. He passed by fish and seaweed as he fell deeper and deeper. It grew cold and dark and he could not breathe. "This is the end of me," he thought. "I should never have tried to run away from the Lord."

But just as Jonah was about to open his mouth and let the sea water drown him, he was swallowed by a great fish. "Ohhh," he moaned. "I will be eaten alive." But the fish's teeth did not touch him. Before Jonah knew what was happening, he was in the huge, dark belly of the fish.

Jonah cried out to the Lord. "I disobeyed you and tried to hide from you. And now you have punished me. But still I trust in you and worship you. Please hear my prayers and forgive me."

For three days and nights Jonah was in the belly of the fish. He prayed almost all the time—except when he was too afraid. It was terribly dark inside the fish, and as it swam through the sea poor Jonah rolled around like a ball. He was cold and hungry and very tired. "Ohhh," moaned Jonah, "I wish I had obeyed God. I wish I could go home."

Finally, after three days, the fish spit Jonah out on a sandy shore. Jonah could hardly stand up. His knees were weak and his eyes were hurt by the light. He looked terrible! His clothes were torn, his hair was dirty, and he was shaking all over.

Then God spoke to Jonah a second time. "Go to Nineveh and tell the people there that I will destroy their city in forty days."

This time Jonah hurried to do what God told him. For three days he traveled through the mountains and the desert, and when he came to Nineveh he cried, "I have been sent by the Lord. There is much wickedness in Nineveh and this must be punished. In forty days the Lord will destroy your city."

The people of Nineveh knew of the Lord's power and believed what Jonah said. "What shall we do?" they cried fearfully. "We must not let this terrible thing happen. But how can we stop it?"

Then the people hurried to their king and told him what Jonah had said. "Please do something to save us," they begged him.

The king also became afraid. He ordered everyone in Nineveh to put on rough sackcloth and ask for forgiveness. "We must fast," he said. "No man or woman, no child or animal shall eat or drink anything. Also, we must give up our evil habits. We must all be sorry and ask the Lord to forgive us. Then perhaps He will not destroy Nineveh."

When God heard the people of Nineveh ask for forgiveness, He was pleased. And when He saw that they had changed their wicked ways, He was no longer angry with them. And so forty days passed, but God did not destroy Nineveh.

But when Jonah saw that Nineveh was saved, he was angry. "I knew this would happen," he complained to the Lord. "I knew that you are too kind and that you would not really destroy Nineveh. That was why I did not want to come here and why I ran away. Why did you make me come here? You should have destroyed Nineveh. You forgive too much!" And as Jonah said these words he shook his fist and stamped his foot on the ground.

Then Jonah walked to a hill outside Nineveh. He wanted to see if God would change His mind and destroy the city after all. To make himself more comfortable, Jonah built a small shelter. Then he waited to see what would happen to Nineveh.

While Jonah was watching from his hill, God caused a large plant to grow over his head. Jonah was very grateful for the plant because it protected him from the hot sun.

But then a worm began to eat the plant, and before long the plant died. Now Jonah was even more upset. "Why did you let a worm eat the plant?" he demanded of God. "I don't understand you. You didn't destroy the wicked Nineveh, but you killed the beautiful plant which protected me from the sun. Surely it is best for me to die. I am too unhappy, and I will never understand your ways.

Then God said to Jonah, "You are angry and unhappy because I have destroyed the plant? But what did you do to make the plant grow? Did you water it? Did you give it any food? Did you make its vine green?

"No," answered Jonah. "I did none of these things."

"Then think of Nineveh," said the Lord. "I built this city. I gave its people life and I watched it grow to a city of great beauty. The people of Nineveh do not know good from bad, but I have worked a long time to teach them. You feel sorry for a plant that grew in one night, and yet you did nothing for it. How do you think I would feel to see Nineveh destroyed when I cared for it so much and worked for it so long?"

Then Jonah understood. And he felt foolish. He knew he should not have been angry when God did not destroy Nineveh. "I was wrong," Jonah said. "And I have learned two things. No one can escape from the Lord, and no one is more wise or merciful than He is."